April

Ellen Jackson

Illustrated by Kay Life

Charlesbridge

To Pamela Barnes with thanks
—E. J.

To the Carrot Top Kid.
I love you very much.
—K. L.

Sayings, Symbols, and Superstitions

April is a month of melody. In April, you can hear the warbling of mockingbirds and the chattering of squirrels. Frogs croak from pools and streams. Rain splatters on the sidewalk.

Thomas Tusser, an English author, wrote: "Sweet April showers / Do spring May flowers." In many parts of North America, the rains of April soak the earth and nourish young growing plants.

When these April showers come,
animals and people look for shelter.
Insects scurry under leaves or disappear
into holes, and birds ruffle their feathers
to keep the water out.

Squirrels hide under their
bushy tails. In the city, people
huddle under bobbing umbrellas.

April is courtship time for many animals. In Alaska, male grizzly bears challenge each other to fight. The strongest males will win the right to mate with the females. In the mountains, pairs of male and female eagles fly toward each other again and again. They dip, turn, and soar in the air.

People, too, think of romance in April. The famous English poet Alfred, Lord Tennyson, wrote, "In the Spring a young man's fancy lightly turns to thoughts of love." Boys gather flowers for their girlfriends in April. Girls chant, "He loves me . . . he loves me not . . ." as they pluck petals from a daisy.

Eggs are everywhere this time of year.
Fish eggs are coated with a jellylike
substance, while turtle and snake eggs
have a leathery feel. Bird eggs have hard
shells. Ostrich eggs are so strong that a
grown man can stand on one without
breaking it. But all eggs serve the
same purpose. They supply
food and protection to the
growing embryo inside.

The April Birthstone

The birthstone for April is the diamond. This precious gem is usually colorless, although it reflects a rainbow of colors. Sometimes colored diamonds are found. These can be blue, apple green, pink, yellow, and even black. Two famous colored diamonds are the Hope, a blue diamond, and the Tiffany, a yellow diamond that looks like a crystal of golden sunshine.

the Hope Diamond

The April Flower

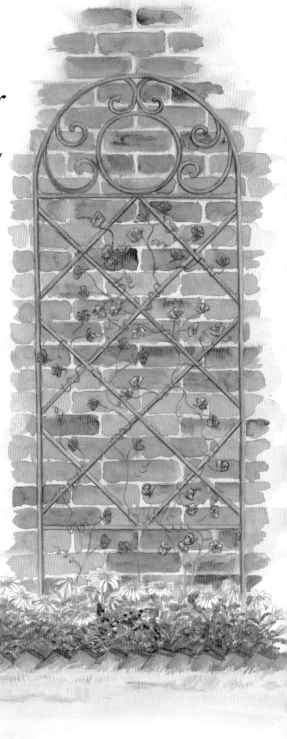

If you were born in April, your special flowers are the sweet pea, a flower noted for its perfume, and the daisy. In Wales, daisies were once used to treat smallpox and to remove warts. In fifteenth-century England, they were sometimes put in salads.

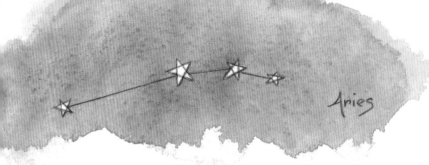

The April Zodiac

Aries, the ram, is the astrological sign for people with birthdays from March 21 to April 19. People born under Aries are said to be bold, courageous, and energetic—the qualities of the ram. They may get angry easily but are also quick to forgive. An Aries is usually affectionate and enjoys finding new ways of doing things.

The sign for people born from April 20 to May 20 is Taurus, the bull. Those born under Taurus are said to be stubborn, somewhat shy, and strong and healthy like the bull. A Taurus is also thought to be musical, artistic, and a hard worker.

The Calendar

April is the fourth month of the year. It now has thirty days, but this was not always the case. It is said that the rulers of ancient Rome changed the number of days in April back and forth several times. Finally Julius Caesar, one of these rulers, gave it thirty days once and for all.

The name *April* may come from the Latin word *aperire*, which means "to open." In the Northern Hemisphere, April is the month in which buds open and flowers begin to bloom.

Sun, Sky, and Weather

April brings sunlight, breezes, and the rush of flowing water. As the snow melts away, April rain collects on leaves and makes puddles on the ground. In the woods, the earth appears to turn green overnight.

April weather can be quite unpredictable. A sudden hailstorm may clatter on the roof. A few hours later, the warm sun may have melted all the ice. In northern regions, snow still falls from time to time, but in the South, spring flowers are in bloom.

In the Midwest, April is a month for tornadoes. Tornadoes are black, swirling funnels of air that sweep up everything in their path. They tend to occur when warm, moist air collides with cool, dry air.

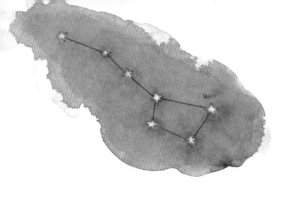

Look to the south on an April night and you can see Regulus, a bright spring star. It is part of the constellation of Leo, the Lion. Northward from Regulus is the Big Dipper. The Big Dipper is higher in April and May than at any other time of year.

The April full moon has been called the grass moon by some Native American peoples of the Northeast. The Anglo-Saxons, who settled in Britain in the fifth and sixth centuries, called April *Eostre monath*, which means "Easter month."

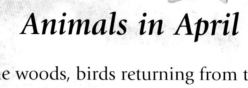

Animals in April

In the woods, birds returning from the south feast on earthworms, ants, and sow bugs. Bumblebee queens begin to build nests and lay eggs in logs or holes in the ground. Newly hatched tent caterpillars spin little silk tents on wild cherry branches.

Snails and slugs come out of hiding after spring rains. Snails lay down a film of mucus as they move over the earth. The mucus helps protect them from rough surfaces, allowing them to travel across an object as sharp as a razor's edge without being hurt.

Wood frogs and spring peepers have been singing since March, but in April they are joined by leopard frogs and toads that are awake after their winter sleep.

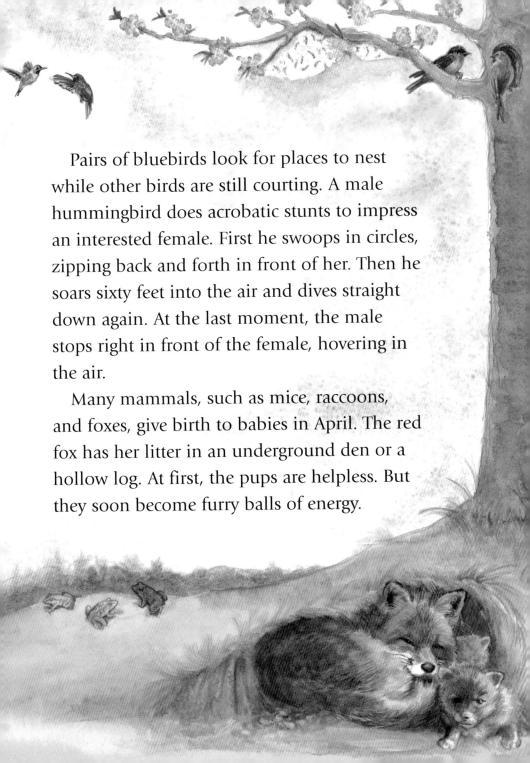

Pairs of bluebirds look for places to nest while other birds are still courting. A male hummingbird does acrobatic stunts to impress an interested female. First he swoops in circles, zipping back and forth in front of her. Then he soars sixty feet into the air and dives straight down again. At the last moment, the male stops right in front of the female, hovering in the air.

Many mammals, such as mice, raccoons, and foxes, give birth to babies in April. The red fox has her litter in an underground den or a hollow log. At first, the pups are helpless. But they soon become furry balls of energy.

River animals are also raising their families in April. The muskrat teaches her young a clever trick for gathering mussels. She spreads the mussel shells in the sunshine and waits for them to dry. Sometimes she turns them over. Soon the drying shells open and she is able to scoop out the insides.

In city parks, pigeons look for mates. The male pigeon likes to play hard-to-get. First he calls: "Roo roo roo." He puffs up his neck feathers and spreads his tail, trying to attract the attention of a female. When one approaches, the male chases her away. But she keeps returning until the male accepts her.

In the spring, desert tortoises can be found feeding on grasses and plants that have not been eaten by cattle and other animals. When the weather gets warmer, they will stay in underground dens to avoid the heat.

Spring on the prairie is also a time of courtship and new life. Bison give birth to their calves in April and May. Prairie chickens do courting dances. The males arrive first, just before sunrise, to claim their territory. At dawn the dances begin. The male birds beat their feet in rhythm on the ground. Then they stop to give a piercing call that can be heard a mile away. Eventually the females select their mates, and the pairs choose nesting sites in meadows or under shrubs.

Plants in April

Some plants, such as violets and crocuses, wait to flower until the light and temperature are just right. Certain plant seeds are coated with chemicals that keep them from growing too early in the year. These chemicals are washed off when just the right amount of rain has fallen. Then the seeds sprout and begin to grow.

In the spring, pollen is in the air. Plants make seeds when pollen from the male part of the flower is carried to the female part. This process is called pollination. Some trees and many flowers depend on insects to spread their pollen. Most forest trees have very small flowers, so their pollen is carried by the wind.

The forest in April smells of fresh water and rotting leaves. Anemones and waxen white bloodroots bloom in the woods. Dogwood trees are bright with white flowers and green leaves. Bluets appear in fields, meadows, and open woods.

In the desert, poppies begin to fade, closing tightly against the blustery wind. Ridges of yellow brittlebush blossoms grow on the hillsides. The brittlebush looks like a green pincushion with stalks that end in an explosion of flowers. Aphids, tiny insects that live on the sap of plants, collect on the flower stalks of the brittlebush. Ladybugs dine on the aphids. Then birds and lizards eat the ladybugs.

Every inch of prairie soil contains a mass of roots. Trees have a hard time finding enough space to get started, so there are few of them to be seen. Much of the rain that falls collects on the grass and never reaches the ground. If you walk through prairie grass after an April storm, you will get soaked with water.

In the city, weeds grow and take over empty lots. Dandelions, chickweed, and thistles are everywhere. It is fun to pick a dandelion, make a wish, and blow the seeds into the wind. The seeds float away on the wind in a ball of fluff.

Special Days

April Fools' Day

April Fools' Day is celebrated in many parts of the world. In India it takes place on March 31 and is called Holi. In France it is called April Fish.

No one knows for certain how it began, but people have been playing April Fools tricks for four hundred years. April Fools' Day may have started when Pope Gregory XIII introduced a new calendar in 1582. This new calendar changed the first day of the New Year from late in March to January 1. People who continued to celebrate the New Year by giving gifts on April 1, as had been the custom, were made fun of and called April fools.

Easter

Christians all over the world celebrate the resurrection of Jesus on Easter Sunday. It is a day of happiness and rejoicing. Many Christians attend sunrise services, gathering in churches, in the mountains, or beside lakes, streams, and oceans on this special day.

The egg has always been a symbol of hope and new life. On Easter, eggs are dyed in beautiful pastel colors. Children hunt for hidden Easter eggs, and people give Easter baskets to one another. Egg rolling is another ancient Easter custom. Children roll eggs down a grassy slope or across a lawn. The winner is the child whose egg crosses the finish line first.

Passover

Passover is a Jewish holiday that lasts for eight days and often falls in early April. During the beginning of Passover, Jews prepare a special dinner called a seder. This dinner commemorates the time when Moses led the Jews out of Egypt. At the seder, the story of the Jew's escape from slavery is retold. People sing Passover songs and eat special foods that symbolize parts of the story.

Famous April Events

On April 9, 1865, the American Civil War came to an end when General Robert E. Lee surrendered to General Ulysses S. Grant, commander in chief of the Union army. All the Union officers removed their hats to honor Lee as he rode away after surrendering. In spite of the Confederate army's defeat, Robert E. Lee was greatly admired in both the North and the South for his courage and dignity. His rival, Ulysses S. Grant, later became the eighteenth president of the United States.

On April 14, 1912, at a few minutes before midnight, the *Titanic*, then the world's largest ocean liner, struck an iceberg. A few hours later it sank into the icy North Atlantic. No one believed the mighty ship could sink, so lifeboats had been provided for only half the passengers. The orchestra continued to play, and many people ignored the danger until the last possible moment. Fifteen hundred men, women, and children drowned in the disaster.

On April 12, 1934, a fierce wind occurred at the Mount Washington Observatory in New Hampshire. Gusts from the wind were recorded at 231 miles an hour. This was the strongest natural wind ever observed on the earth.

On April 12, 1955, the Salk vaccine was first released in the United States. For the first half of the century, poliomyelitis (polio, or infantile paralysis) was one of the most terrifying diseases to strike young people. The vaccine, named after its developer Jonas Salk, almost wiped out polio. In 1977, Jonas Salk was awarded the Presidential Medal of Freedom.

On April 12, 1961, Yuri Gagarin, a Russian cosmonaut, became the first man in space. Gagarin orbited the earth for 108 minutes in *Vostok I*, a spaceship launched from the Soviet Union. On his return, he was given a hero's welcome.

Birthdays

Many famous people were born in April.

April 2, 1805

Author of such popular fairy tales as "The Emperor's New Clothes" and "The Ugly Duckling."

April 4, 1928

Poet, playwright, performer, and author.

April 5, 1856

Educator, author, and founder of Tuskegee University.

April 5, 1937

Secretary of State under George W. Bush. Former U.S. Army general and chairman of the Joint Chiefs of Staff.

Thomas Jefferson

April 13, 1743

Third president of the
United States and author
of the Declaration
of Independence.

Pete Rose

April 14, 1941

Baseball player and
record-breaking hitter.

Charlie Chaplin

April 16, 1889

Silent film comedian
most famous for his
role as the little tramp,
a character with baggy
pants, big shoes, and
an awkward walk.

Charlotte Brönte

April 21, 1816

Author of *Jane Eyre*
and other novels.

William Shakespeare

April 23, 1564

English playwright, poet,
and author of *Hamlet*,
Romeo and Juliet, *King
Lear*, and *Macbeth*.

Shirley Temple Black

April 23, 1928

1930s child movie star,
who became a delegate
to the United Nations.

An April Story

People used to see a man they called "Johnny Appleseed" paddling up and down the Wabash river with two canoes tied together. One of the canoes held sacks of apple seeds. Whenever Johnny came to a region that had recently been settled, he would plant his seeds or give them to the settlers. He seldom asked for money, but he would sometimes trade the seeds for food and clothing.

Johnny was not a fancy dresser. He wore an old coffee sack with holes cut in it for his head and arms. On his head he wore the tin pan with which he cooked. He refused to buy shoes, so he usually went barefoot.

Johnny gave out apple seeds because he thought cutting trees to graft buds was cruel. In fact, Johnny was concerned for all living creatures. A wolf he had freed from a trap kept him company for years. Johnny talked aloud to the birds and animals as he walked across the country. Once he killed a snake by accident, and for years he cried whenever he remembered what he had done.

To this day, many people in Pennsylvania and Indiana can point to apple trees descended from those Johnny Appleseed planted more than two hundred years ago.

AUTHOR'S NOTE

This book gives an overview of the month of April in North America. But nature does not follow a strict schedule. The mating and migration of animals, the blooming of plants, and other natural events vary from year to year, or occur earlier or later in different places.

The zodiac section of this book is included just for fun. The April personalities are part of the folklore of the month and should not be taken as accurate descriptions of any real people.

The story of Johnny Appleseed was adapted from *American Folklore and Legend*, edited by Jane Polley. (New York: Reader's Digest Association, 1978.)

Text copyright © 2002 by Ellen Jackson
Illustrations copyright © 2002 by Kay Life
All rights reserved, including the right of reproduction in whole or in part in any form.

Published by Charlesbridge Publishing
85 Main Street, Watertown, MA 02472
(617) 926-0329
www.charlesbridge.com

Illustrations done in watercolor on Fabriano hot press paper
Display type and text type set in Giovanni
Color separations made by Sung In Printing, South Korea
Printed and bound by Sung In Printing, South Korea
Production supervision by Brian G. Walker
Designed by Diane M. Earley

Cataloging-in-Publication Data is available upon request

Printed in South Korea
10 9 8 7 6 5 4 3 2 1